751192

MIDLOTHIAN D

WITHD

AF574703

ROCKETS
General Editor: AIDAN CHAMBERS

Snake River

Aidan Chambers

751192
5

Macmillan Education

© Aidan Chambers 1975, 1977

All rights reserved. No part
of this publication may be reproduced
or transmitted, in any form or by any
means, without permission

First published 1975
by Almqvist & Wiksell, Sweden

First published in Rockets 1977

Published by
MACMILLAN EDUCATION LTD
Houndmills Basingstoke Hampshire RG21 2XS
and London
Associated companies in New York Dublin
Melbourne Johannesburg and Delhi

Printed in Hong Kong

Illustrator: Peter Morgan

Chambers, Aidan Snake river. – (Rockets). ISBN 0–333–21524–9
1. Title 2. Series 428′.6′2 PE1126.D4 Readers

1

The morning the trouble started, I was high up the valley above our cabin staking out a new field. When I rested from pounding away at the wooden fence poles, I looked over the dark green pine trees which hid our cabin from view, down the valley to Calpet. The clustered frame houses of the town were bright in the sharp spring sunlight, and seemed nearer than they were.

Spring had pushed the snow out of the valley, but the air was still frost-cold when it blew off the snow-capped mountains. I spat on my hands. The stakes were jarring in the stony ground. Every fall of the heavy sledgehammer sent tingles up my arms. I had been at it all morning. Pa wanted more land cleared. He wanted to grow beet. The cattle men had found a taste for it, and the market would be high this year.

Ours was the last claim up the valley. We'd come there when I was three years old. Pa chose it because he wanted to be out of the way of the cattle men, who disliked us farmers. He was a solitary man, too, and valued his privacy. Apart from Ma and me, he hardly saw anybody, month in, month out.

I used to wish we had more company sometimes. Then I'd ride down to Calpet on the excuse of buying supplies. Calpet was at the foot of the valley, where the farmer's claims ended and the cattle ranches began. After Calpet there was nothing but waves of grassland spreading into the distance, endless.

Calpet was a quiet place. It was so quiet some folks grumbled about paying the tax for the sheriff's wage. There had been no trouble for years. An occasional fight, maybe, when the cowpunchers came into town from a long range ride and wanted some fun. But nothing anybody called trouble. Life had got so peaceful that the townsfolk had even built a church. They had a school planned, too, and a woman from back east was coming to teach there.

I was eighteen that year, and glad to be too old for school. Ma used to teach me at home when I was a boy, and that was bad enough. She gave up trying to teach me book lessons when I was fourteen. Pa gave me Silva on my birthday. I rode him all that day, till the froth was white on his bit and his hide was shining with sweat. When I got home, Pa said, 'That horse ain't just a plaything, boy. It's time you did man's work. You'll need that horse to do it.'

I took a rest from pounding the fence stakes, and went over to Silva and took a drink from my water bottle. It tasted sweet and good. There's nothing as sharp and cool and refreshing as mountain water in spring.

I stood there savouring the water in my mouth and looking at Calpet shimmering in the hazy warmth of the sunlight. Maybe if Calpet hadn't been such a peaceful place for so long, things would have happened differently. When there has been no trouble in a place for years, people get to thinking none will ever come again. When it does, it takes everybody by surprise.

I was hanging the water bottle back on my saddle when I heard the shots. I thought maybe someone was hunting, or perhaps a stray cowboy was letting off some steam. I looked down the valley in idle curiosity: there might be some fun to see. Cowhands get up to queer antics.

More shots rang out, echoes from the mountain repeating the sounds. Puffs of gunsmoke were rising like little white clouds above the trees where our cabin lay. I stiffened. They spelt trouble to me, just as clear as if they had been Indian war signals. Everybody in Calpet knew my pa wouldn't allow guns on the claim. Pa thought guns were weapons of the Devil. He wouldn't even use one to kill pests. It was all Ma and me could do to get him to kill pests by any means at all. 'All life is sacred to the Lord,' he'd say, and there was no good in arguing with him. If Pa had his way, we would stand by while woodchucks ate the heart out of the crops. That didn't make sense to me: made me go hot with anger.

While I stood watching, three more puffs ballooned into the air, and three more shots echoed up the valley. I swung into the saddle and dug my spurs into Silva.

As I came in sight of the cabin, two men went riding off fast down the trail to Calpet. They rode like cowhands after a night in town: wild and reckless.

I found Pa by the barn at the back of the cabin. He was slumped over a pile of hay, his body twisted strangely and a rope binding his feet together in a noose. Ma was bending over him. She heard me coming and ran to me. She was weeping and her eyes were wide with fear.

'Your pa,' she said. 'He's hurt bad, Clint!'

I swung down from Silva and ran to him. He was breathing, but painfully, and it only took a glance to see his right arm was broken. He had bruises on the right side of his head too, some of them bleeding. He was unconscious. He was a big man, my pa. Up to that day, I had never seen him ill. Now, the sight of him lying there, crumpled up and unconscious, seemed like an insult to him: like a fine healthy tree felled for no reason.

'Help me lift him, Clint,' Ma said. Together we got him as gently as we could into the house where we laid him on his bed.

'Get something to make splints, son,' Ma said.

I went to the barn and found some pieces of wood that were pliant but strong enough, and took them into the house. Ma was tearing a sheet into strips for bandages. She was struggling with herself, now and then brushing tears from her eyes with her hands, and trying to stay calm.

While she bound Pa's arm, I questioned her, and managed to piece the story together.

Seems like two men came up to the cabin. They were strangers and looked like brothers. They were dusty, too, as though they had been living rough for a long time. They wanted food and a bed for the night. Pa took one look at the guns they had slung on them, and the rifles on their saddles, and said 'No'. Guns worked like a spur on a stallion to Pa: nothing made him lose his temper faster.

The two men got rough. They tried to make fun of Pa first, but that got them nowhere. Then, one of the men distracted him. The other sprung out a lasso and grounded him as though he were hobbling a steer. They pulled Pa over to the barn and hoisted him from a beam in the roof. They pulled him up feet-first on the end of the rope until he was dangling head down about twenty feet from the ground. They took their pistols out and said they'd show him what a good gunman could do. They started shooting at the rope just above his feet. They treated it all like a game, Ma said, taking it in turns and betting between

them as to which one would shoot the rope in two. Finally, one of them hit the rope and parted it. Pa fell head first to the ground.

They left him lying there and forced Ma to give them food. They stuffed the food into their saddle bags, and rode off. By then Pa had crawled to the hay before he collapsed. Ma got to him just before I rode in.

It was middle afternoon before we got Pa straightened out and comfortable. All his right side was badly grazed and bruised, and there were welts round his ankles where the rope had cut into the flesh.

Pa came to soon afterwards. He was dazed and in considerable pain. When I saw he was conscious and that Ma was feeling more calm and had got over the shock, I said to her:

'I'm going into Calpet to see about those two wildcats.'

Pa heard. 'Leave them be, boy,' he said. It was painful just to hear the strain in his voice. I went to him.

'I can't do that, Pa,' I said. 'I just can't let men get away with things like this.'

'Clint,' Pa said, 'I ain't never turned my hand against any man. Never have, and never will. That's the way I live, and I ain't changing now just because somebody roughed me up.'

'Roughed you up! They near killed you for no reason except mean-minded spite.'

'That's as may be, son. But I tell you, you ain't to do anything about it, understand?'

He was just the same now as he was about the woodchucks and blue jays and all the other pests. Even though he was lying there, beaten up and hurt, he made me boil inside with anger.

'I'm sorry, Pa,' I said. 'This time I'm not listening.'

I made for the door. Pa growled, and tried to move, and yelled at the hurt of trying, and lay back again. Ma blocked my way to the door.

'Don't go, Clint,' she said. 'You can't handle men like that. They're heartless, Clint. They'll do as bad by you as they have by your father.'

It was harder talking against her: it always is against women. 'Look, Ma,' I said, 'I'm not going to take them on by myself. The sheriff can handle it. It's his job. But I'm not letting them get away with what they've done, neither. It isn't right.'

'Just now, son,' Ma said, 'I'm not much interested in right and wrong. I don't want you getting hurt like your father.'

'I'll be fine, Ma,' I said, gentle as I could. 'You take care of Pa. I'll be back in no time.'

I went out and got Silva and rode off, heading for Calpet and the sheriff's office. I didn't look back because I knew Ma was standing weeping at the door.

2

Old Jake Barnes was sitting outside the sheriff's office. Jake ran the livery stable. But he was more often sitting in the sun outside the sheriff's place than next door in his stable. A place like Calpet, being off the main trails, didn't get many visitors, so there was little call for the livery. Jake lived in the loft above the stables and made himself a few extra pennies by doing odd jobs round the town.

Most people liked the old guy. He had a way of telling a story, while he scratched at his stubbled beard and looked at you with a twinkle in his eye, that nobody could help liking. If you wanted to know anything that was going on in town, you asked Jake. Having so little to do, and always sitting round the sheriff's place, he picked up the news as soon as it happened. Some folk said Jake knew the news before the news had happened.

'Hello, there!' Jake said.

'Hi, Jake,' I said, and went straight by him into the sheriff's. The office was empty. I went to the door.

'You seen the sheriff, Jake?'

'Yes, I seen him,' Jake said.

'Do you know where he is?'

'Sure do.'

'Well where, Jake?'

'Out of town. Gone to Pinedale.'

'Pinedale! That's a day's ride. What's he doing there?'

'Seeing a friend of his get married, so I believe.' Jake pushed his hat back from his eyes and looked up at me, smiling. 'You in some kind of trouble?'

'You could say! When's the sheriff due back?'

'Tomorrow. Maybe the day after. Depends how much talking and drinking gets to be done. Mighty unpredictable things, weddings. Sometimes get stretched longer than was meant.'

I leaned against the door post. Jake got up from his chair in his slow, old man's way, and stood in front of me. I was thinking, paying no attention to him, wondering what to do next. Jake stood facing me a while, grinning. Then he started puffing his chest out and rubbing something pinned to his vest. When he stopped rubbing, I saw he was wearing a deputy sheriff's badge, shining bright.

'Thought you'd never notice,' Jake said. 'You can talk to me, if you like.' He was as proud as if he was a US Marshal. 'Sheriff deputised me yesterday, just before he left for that there wedding.'

Now, Jake couldn't read or write, and he had arthritis so bad you could almost hear him creak when he walked. Him being sheriff was just about the biggest joke this side of Laramie. And ordinarily I would have laughed along with everybody else. But not now.

'That's crazy,' I said. 'You aren't capable.'

'Young fella, you just watch what you're saying there. You're talking to the Calpet deputy, and I don't take no insults.' He was grinning and scratching his beard, his eyes twinkling in the shade of his floppy old hat. He thought the sheriff's badge as big a joke as everyone else did. 'It's like the sheriff said when he offered me the job. "Jake," he says to me, "Jake, who knows more about everything in this town than anybody else? You!" he says. "And who has more time on his hands than any other man for miles hereabout? You!" he says. "And who knows the workings of this doggone sheriff's office better than the sheriff himself? You!" he says. "So there doesn't seem anybody better fitted to sit outside and watch the world stroll by in this one-horse, peace-loving community than you." And with that he raises my right hand, swears me to Heaven to dish out law and order, and slaps this badge on my chest.'

Old Jake was laughing so much he had to sit down again. He slapped his knee, looked at me sideways and said: 'Besides – I can use the money!' He roared louder than ever. 'Three dollars,' he laughed. 'Three round solid, silver dollars I get for sitting here in the sun and passing the time of day with whomever has the time to pass and something to say! Never got so well paid in my life for doing what I do all day long anyway!'

I stood there and listened, and waited until Jake had got through his laughter.

Then I said, 'You'd best come inside, Jake. I got some news to tell you.'

By the time I finished telling Jake what had happened, there was no more laughter in him. He sat behind the sheriff's desk, slumped in the chair, as glum as a cowpuncher on the winter range.

'Have you seen two strangers today, Jake?' I asked.

He nodded. 'Wondered why they came into town looking so frisky. Matter of fact, they're still here – over in the saloon. That's their two horses outside.'

I looked through the office window at the horses tethered outside the saloon just up the street. They were dusty and had Texas saddles with red and white Navaho

saddle blankets. Bed rolls were tied behind the saddles. They were big beasts, bigger than cowhands normally like. Those two were built for travelling, not for cutting out steers, and were just the kind of horse footloose riders choose.

I turned to Jake. 'OK,' I said. 'Let's go.'

'Go?' Jake said. 'Go where?'

'Why, across to the saloon. Nobody else has come through here today. It must be them.'

'Now hold on there, young Clint. Are you suggesting I go over there and take those men?'

'You're the sheriff, Jake. Have you got another plan?'

'I ain't got no plan at all! Except to go on sitting right here.'

I was getting real angry. 'You mean you're just going to sit there and let those two wildcats get away?'

Jake got up and started pacing round the room. 'Don't see what else I can do. Ain't any evidence they did it anyway.'

'No evidence!' I shouted. 'Well, you just fetch them in, and I'll soon show you evidence!'

Jake got agitated. 'I can't go over there, Clint. Have you seen those two? I can't handle fellas like that. They're gunslingers. You think they're going to come in here meek as lambs and let me lock them up? They'd mess me up twice as bad as they did your pa if I tried. I'm no gunman, Clint, I never have been; and I'm too old to start now.'

I watched that old man pleading with me, and jittering about the office with his deputy's badge shining on his chest, and I didn't know whether to feel pity or plain disgust. He finished talking, leaning against the desk with his back to me.

'You should have thought about that before you took the badge,' I said.

He turned and came up to me.

'I know how you feel, son,' he said. 'I'd be the same way in the circumstances. But nobody expected anything like this in Calpet. Sheriff wouldn't have gone off to Pinedale if he had. He only deputised me because he wanted to do me a good turn. Knew I could use the extra money.'

'Well, Jake,' I said, 'you've got the badge and you've taken the money, and now you've got trouble. I don't reckon to let those two men get away with what they've done to my pa, so you'd better start thinking fast.'

'I tell you, there ain't anything I can do.'

'Then if you won't, maybe there's others will. I'm going over there, Jake, and I'm going to face those two with what they've done.'

Old Jake took hold of me. 'Don't be a fool, boy. You can't handle them men on your own.'

'Maybe not,' I said. 'But if the other men in that saloon have anything about them, they might help. They know my pa. And they know what happened to him could happen to them.'

'Who's going to stand up against two gunslingers, Clint? Talk sense. You can't do no good, and maybe will do a lot of harm. What are you going to do when you get there? Ask them nice and polite to step over to the sheriff's and be locked up?'

'Let me go, Jake.'

'Wait till the sheriff gets back. He'll deal with them.'

'And do you think those men are going to hang about waiting for him?'

'We could send for him. We could send for him and get

him back here. He could be in town by tomorrow morning.'

'That isn't good enough for me, Jake. Once they get clear of town, they won't aim to let a sheriff catch up with them. So you just clear out of my way.'

I pushed past Jake and went out of the office, and walked over to the saloon.

3

When I stepped into the saloon, thirteen pairs of eyes turned to look. Six men were playing poker at a table. Joe was behind the bar pouring whisky. Six men stood at the bar. Four of them I knew by sight: they were cowhands from the Lazy Y ranch. But two I had never seen before. I knew from Ma's description they were the ones I was looking for.

They weren't tall – about five feet seven – but they were heavily built. Their blue levis stretched on their legs. They both wore brown corduroy vests over blue shirts. The vests were faded from age and dust and weather. They were brothers sure enough. They had the same blue eyes, so pale they looked nearly white; the same thick long noses. Two-day beards made their faces dark. Sweat-stained stetson hats were pushed back, showing jet-black hair. One of them had a scar from the lobe of his ear running down under his collar. When they saw me, they grinned at each other.

Joe was flashing looks between me and the two men, uneasy looks that showed he knew more than he should. I had the feeling they had all been laughing about something just before I came in.

Joe said, 'Thought yours was a temperance family, Clint.'

'You thought right, Joe,' I said, keeping my eyes on the

strangers. Joe took a cloth and started rubbing the bar top. 'What can I get you?' he said.

'Nothing, Joe. Nothing at all.'

All this time, the brothers were eyeing me up and down in a slow deliberate way. The one with the scar turned to Joe. 'Thought boys weren't allowed in bars,' he said, and he pitched his voice just loud enough so everybody in the room could hear. Some of the men chuckled.

I looked round at all of them. 'Thought you men might like to know my pa just got beat up by two strangers,' I said.

The men went silent. Only the brothers moved. They put their backs to the bar and leaned against it with their elbows.

'Maybe you ought to call the sheriff,' Scarface said.

'He's out of town,' I said. I looked round at the others. 'Thought, maybe, you men would help put things right.'

At that Joe went to rubbing the bar top hard enough to take the polish off, and every face turned away from me. Some seemed to find specks on their hands that needed picking at; others played with their drinks, or the cards on the table. Only the brothers kept their eyes on me.

The one without the scar said, 'That's too bad, kid.'

'Brother George,' Scarface said, 'we ought to buy the boy a drink.'

'We should?' George replied.

'The boy must be shocked after such a thing,' Scarface said. 'He needs somthing to steady him.'

'Why, brother Ben, you're right,' George said. 'A man can't think straight after a shock like that.'

I took a step towards them.

'I say it was you two beat up my pa,' I said.

Joe stopped polishing. Ben leaned off the bar and stood square on his feet.

'I say you're wrong . . . kid,' he said.

George laid a hand on Ben's arm. 'The kid's confused, brother. It's the shock and all. He needs a drink.'

'I'm thinking he needs something more than a drink, brother,' Ben said. 'Something that might teach him to speak more careful.'

'He's only a boy, Ben,' George said. 'Ain't even old enough to carry a gun.'

Ben relaxed, and the smile came back on his face, one of those mocking, superior smiles that are so annoying.

'Why, that's true, brother,' he said. 'And he's so thin a gunbelt would slip straight down to his feet and trip him up!'

He looked round at the others. Nobody moved. Some of the men looked up at him, and smiled. 'What do you say, men? The kid's confused, eh? Needs something to steady him.'

There was silence. Ben laid his hand casually on his holster. 'Now I ask you,' he said, grinning. 'Do George and me look like men who would beat up the kid's pa?'

He laughed loudly, but his body was still square on his feet, and his hand rested on his gun. One or two men smiled, then forced a laugh.

Ben looked at George. George took up the laughter, and so it grew among them as though the meaning of a good joke was just coming clear in their minds.

'Let's give him a drink, eh?' shouted Ben.

'Yeah,' some of the men shouted back. 'Let's see him have a drink.'

Ben came towards me, with George following a step behind.

'We don't take offence from what *boys* say!' Ben said. The men roared again. 'What have we done to get offended about anyways?' And that caused another wave of laughter.

Ben got a step in front of me, and the anger in my stomach rose. I hit out at his grinning face.

He grabbed my wrist with a hard thick hand and pulled. I lurched forward. Ben hung on to my right arm, and George stepped aside and caught hold of my left. They drew me against the bar. George twisted my arm behind me, took the other from Ben and brought that up behind me too. Then he pulled backwards and turned me so I faced the other men. Ben took the whisky bottle from the bar in one hand; with the other he took a fistful of hair and pulled my head back till my mouth was forced open. He tipped the bottle, letting the whisky stream into my mouth.

I spluttered and choked and began to thrash about, kicking my legs wildly and struggling. George hung on, and together we careered round the room, knocking furniture from our path.

'Why – the boy's dancing,' I heard Ben shout.

George got me back to the bar and held me down over it. Ben tipped the bottle again. The whisky splashed over my head and face. It got into my eyes where it stung and burned. It ran into my ears and muffled the shouts and laughter in the room.

I was struggling like a wild thing now, but George held on, and the whisky blinded me from seeing where my feet were kicking.

'Joe,' Ben shouted, 'you shouldn't allow boys in this bar. If the sheriff was in town, he'd be mighty disapproving. We'd better help you clear this boy out!'

I felt myself pulled backwards, turned, and then pushed forward so fast my feet couldn't catch up. I was flung away and released. I tumbled, hitting my head against something hard that gave in front of me, and I spilled out into the street, tripping over my own feet and the wood pavement, before I fell in the dust of the road.

I lay there a minute, catching my breath, my eyes stinging. I tried to rub them, but grit from the road was on my hands. It got into my eyes, which hurt more. My face and chest were bruised, and I felt sick in my stomach from the liquor I'd swallowed. And through it all I could hear the laughter going on in the saloon.

Suddenly, I was hauled off the ground.

'Told you not to go in there,' said Jake's voice. 'Couldn't do anything but harm.'

Jake guided me to the livery stable, supporting me while I stumbled blindly along. All the way, he chuntered, half to himself, half to me, scolding and sympathising with me and cursing the brothers by turns.

'Suppose it could be a lot worse,' he said, sitting me on some hay in the stable. 'You might be dead.'

4

Jake pushed my head into a bucket of cold water. Pretty soon, the whisky was out of my eyes and I felt better. The bruises were sore, but they would heal. And the better I felt, the worse my temper got.

I dried my hair with some sacking. 'The dirty, no-good, mean-minded sons of a prairie dog,' I raged, giving vent to my pent-up anger. I threw the sacking down and paced round the stable.

'Just calm down,' Jake said. 'There ain't anything you can do. I keep telling you that – but, goddammit, you pay no attention!'

'I won't rest till those two are behind bars.'

'That's no job for you,' Jake said. 'Nor me neither.'

'Well, you'd better think up something, Jake, because if those two wildcats leave town, I'm going after them.'

Jake really got stirred up at that. 'Why you hot-headed, stubborn young mustang,' he shouted. 'You're as cussed as your pa. You're all alike, you Matthews. You get your heads fixed on something and won't budge, even if all hell is let loose. Now you just come over here. I've got something to show you that might make you see sense.'

He took off his sweaty old hat and pulled a folded sheet of paper out of the crown. I went over and sat by him on a bench at the stable door.

'It's common knowledge I can't read nor write,' Jake

said. 'But that don't mean I've got no head on my shoulders.'

I tried to see what the paper was, but Jake held it close to his chest.

'Just bide your time, young fella,' he said, smiling.

'What have you got there, Jake?' I said.

'Well now, keep your patience and I'll tell you.' When Jake had a story, he was never to be rushed. I sat back and listened. 'While you were in Joe's place getting yourself in a mess, I sat outside the sheriff's in the sun, having a think with myself. It weren't too long before it came to me that there was more to them strangers than meets the eye. I got the idea from their horses. They're no cow ponies. They're hard-riding creatures built for power and distance.'

'I'd decided that before I went into the saloon,' I said.

Jake gave me a long look. 'That's as may be,' he said. 'Either way, hold your tongue till I've done.' He spat and shuffled himself comfortable again. 'Long and the short of it is, I went into the sheriff's office and had a glance through his files. Came up with this.'

He handed me the paper. It was a 'Wanted' notice, three years old according to the date on it. It showed the pictures of two men, with their descriptions printed underneath.

'It's them, Jake!' I said.

Jake puffed his chest out. 'Knew so myself! Can't read words, but I can see pictures! But what's the writing say? I've been living with the suspense of what those two outlaws are wanted for, ever since I found that notice. It's enough to drive a man wild having the wherefores and not being able to understand. Even got to wishing I'd spent some time in schooling as a lad.'

I read the notice aloud. The two men were George and Ben Shaw, thirty-four years old, and known sometimes as the Prank Brothers. Seemed they were always playing jokes on people, and that's how they got the name. They were wanted for robbery and murder down in Texas. That's about all the notice said. Except there was a thousand-dollar reward for each one. Dead or alive.

Jake let out a whistle. 'Well, I'll be doggoned!' he said. 'If that don't cool your temper, I can't think what will.'

'Cool my temper, Jake? It just adds wood to the fire!'

'But they're a mighty dangerous pair, boy. They'd put a bullet through you soon as spit!'

I stood up. 'Do you mean you're just going to sit there and do nothing, Jake Barnes, while there's two criminals and two thousand dollars lying in your lap? That's not just cowardice – it's foolishness.'

'Now that's wild, unpleasant talk, young Clint,' Jake said angrily. 'I'm fixing to do something: but I'm not bent on playing the hero. I prefer living poor to dying rich.'

I stalked away from him. 'Well, I think different.'

Jake followed me up the stable and back again, barking at me like an old dog at a steer. 'Then what are you going to do about it?' he said. 'Maybe you're thinking of having a little gunplay with the Shaws? Maybe you see yourself shooting them down and turning their bodies over to the marshal, eh? Being congratulated all round, with speeches and bands playing and your name in the papers? Collecting the reward in a blaze of glory? That it?'

Perhaps that's just what I had been thinking. And Jake saying it like that stung me.

'Then you suggest something else,' I said.

'I'll tell you what I aim to do. I'm riding over to Pinedale to get the sheriff. He can deputise a posse and round up them two outlaws himself.'

UNDERTAKE

'You're just teeming with new ideas, Jake!' I said. 'How do you think those two have kept from being caught all this time? By flitting from place to place, that's how. Nobody ever dares face them square, and by the time a posse gets on the trail after them, they've disappeared.'

Just then there was the sound of hoofs on the road outside. When I got to the door, I saw the Shaws riding out of town, making for the trail that led to the hills.

'There they go now,' I shouted to Jake. 'What did I just tell you? By the time you've got the sheriff, they'll be away and clear.'

It was more than I could bear to see the brothers slipping off. I knew Jake was right. But I knew that by the time the sheriff got back to town and picked up their trail, they would never be caught.

'Jake,' I said, turning to the old man and talking fast, 'you get busy fetching the sheriff. I'm going after those two. Maybe I can lay a trail as I go, so the sheriff has something to work on.'

I ran to Silva, mounted, spurred him after the disappearing figures of the Shaws.

Jake shuffled after me. 'Come back here, Clint Matthews,' he shouted. 'Why, you ain't even got a gun.'

'No time,' I shouted back.

'Nor any food neither,' I heard him call.

I waved back, leaving him standing in the street.

5

The Shaw brothers rode up into the hills and struck out northwards, following the mountains, but keeping well below the treeline. I couldn't think why they chose that direction. There was nothing ahead but rugged country that made travel difficult.

I jogged along, keeping out of sight, and now and then taking a cautious look to see I was still on their trail. It was beautiful up there in the spring sunlight with the brush bursting fresh green, and the mountains standing clear, sharp, their snow-white tops seeming to sail in the blue sky. Silva was good on rough ground. He found his own paths and kept a steady, easy pace.

I marked the way we took by breaking small tree branches every now and then so they pointed the way like arrows. I reckoned the sheriff's posse would catch up faster if they had a clear trail. And a sudden squall like we often had in spring could wash away horse tracks in minutes.

Being on the east face of the mountains, darkness drifted in early. Sometimes, when I got a glimpse from a spur, I would see the sun still bright on the plains miles away. But under the pines the shadows were thick. When dark came, the Shaws stopped in a fold of the hills surrounded by rocks and trees, and bedded down. They had a fire going in next to no time, and the breeze fetched the smell of frying bacon to me. My mouth watered, and my stomach got to rumbling and creaking. I began to wish I'd heeded Jake, and stayed in town long enough to pack some food. It was too early in the year to find berries or anything of that kind to eat; and even if I'd had a gun I wouldn't have been able to shoot some supper, or cook it, for fear the brothers learned I was there. All I could do was lie low, and smell that food cooking, and curse myself for my foolishness.

After supper, the Shaws settled to smoking and talking and laughing together, the sound drifting up to me where I lay watching. The light from the fire enclosed them in a warm cocoon that made me feel the sharp edge of the breeze and the loneliness and the dark all the more. Pretty soon I got to wondering what they were talking about. Seemed to me I would be better off doing something than just lying there, cold and hungry, watching them. So I started to crawl through the brush, edging closer. The moon was shining, a round piece of ice in the sky; it gave me light to see by, and deep blue shadows to hide in. I inched closer and closer, crouching and cat-walking and squirming on my belly, until I was in earshot and smelling the smoke from their fire drifting by me: strong, sweet wood smoke that sometimes stuck in my throat till I wanted to cough. It got so bad near the circle of flickering light that I picked up a pebble from the ground and pushed it into my mouth to suck, so the saliva would flow and keep my throat wet.

The brothers were talking loudly by this time. Ben had brought out a bottle of whisky from his bedroll, and he and George were passing it back and forth between them. Sometimes they'd laugh like crazy, and tumble about on their blankets.

When I'd listened a while, I realised they were talking about what they'd done to Pa, recounting it and making fun of him and how they'd taken turns to shoot him down, and how Ben had been the one to shoot well enough to cut the rope.

'Always was a better shot than you, brother George,' Ben said, as they rolled about in laughter.

'That's a plain lie, Ben Shaw,' George said. 'Why, in Hot Springs it was me shot the hat off the preacher. That's better than you ever came near to.'

Ben just laughed louder. George seemed to sober. 'And I'll tell you something, brother Ben,' he said. You're getting lax. Taking chances more than is wise. I been telling you all afternoon: we should have gone straight on to Jackson, 'stead of playing games round Calpet.'

Ben took a pull on the bottle. 'Brother George, you're getting old,' he said, mocking. 'You're losing your nerve.'

'I just don't see no sense in taking chances when we're so near Jackson. We'll have all the time in the world to have fun there. That boy in Calpet is just the kind to stir up trouble.'

'Why, he was fun!' Ben said. 'The sight of him dancing round that saloon and you hanging on like you were bucking a bronc – that was the best laugh I've had for days!'

'Maybe so,' George said. 'But I'll be glad to ride into Jackson.'

'Two days, brother, and we'll be home and dry. But I'll tell you one thing, brother George. Don't you get soft-headed. Don't you get jittery and feverish about being caught. Because I don't take to that. There ain't nothing worse than a weak-bellied man! Brother!'

That ended their talk. George didn't take the bottle

again. He lay back with his hands behind his head, saying no more. Ben went on swilling the whisky into himself and chuckling.

By now I had cramps from lying so still, and I got to itching in the most painful kind of way in all the places I couldn't scratch without moving and maybe making a noise. I knew all I wanted anyway, to I set off back to where Silva was tethered; and the crawl back seemed longer and harder on my knees and hands than before.

The rest of the night, I lay wrapped in Silva's saddle blanket, looking at the stars and thinking about what I'd heard. Now I knew why the brothers had struck north. I could have kicked myself for not realising before. Jackson was known all over the territory as a hideout for outlaws. It was high up in the mountains, a small town called Jackson Hole on the edge of a high plateau. It was harsh country, difficult to get into. Jackson Hole was so full of gunmen and outlaws that there wasn't a lawman dared go near the place. Once there, the brothers would be as safe as they ever could be.

I pondered all night long how I could hold them up till the sheriff reached us, and got nowhere. And got no sleep, either.

The brothers broke camp just after sunrise. I jogged along behind them, just out of sight. I was so hungry, I thought my backbone would poke through my stomach. I went on pondering schemes to stop the brothers from going farther, but my head kept nodding down on to my chest with sleepiness. And when the sun got up, it was so warm and comforting I couldn't keep my eyes open.

Suddenly I heard a swish through the air, and a rope came down over my shoulders, and the noose was pulled

so tight it cut into my arms and chest. Then it was given a jerk that lifted me out of the saddle and landed me with a bone-shattering thud on the ground.

That woke me all right; but I was dazed from the fall. Before I could recover, I was heaved up from behind and dragged backwards, stumbling and tripping over ruts and scrub until my back collided with a tree, knocking the breath from me again. The rope was passed round me, lashing me to the tree.

Ben and George appeared from behind, one on either side.

'Nice morning for a ride, kid,' Ben said.

I twisted myself. The rope cut farther into me.

'No use wriggling like that, boy,' Ben said. 'You ain't going nowhere anyhow.'

George brought their horses from where they had been hidden. 'Leave him be, Ben. Let's get on,' he said.

Ben turned to him. 'Why, brother,' he said, 'you're real jumpy! I tell you: you're losing your nerve!'

'Don't see no point in fooling round with that kid again,' George said.

Ben looked at him a minute, then laughed: the same laugh he had given me in the saloon.

'Boy,' he said, turning back to me. 'My brother here is mighty nervous. He don't like folk riding along behind him. Sets him all on edge. So I'm going to ask you to stay just where you are for a while. And maybe just help you do that!'

He came up to me. 'Put your gun on the boy, brother George,' he said.

'You're wasting time,' George said flatly.

'George – put your gun on the boy,' Ben said, and he wasn't fooling anymore. His voice was slow and menacing.

George did nothing for a time. Ben looked at him, moving his head slowly in George's direction 'George . . .' he said.

George took out his gun and aimed at me.

'Now – hold still, boy,' Ben said. He bent down and pulled off my boots, then stood and flung them away behind me. I heard them crash through branches before they landed.

He went up to Silva, turned him down the trail we had just come along, and beat him hard on the flank. Silva took off at a gallop.

'Let's go,' George said.

Ben laughed. 'Ain't done yet,' he said. He mounted his horse, rode up the trail a few yards and wheeled round to face me. Slowly, he drew his gun from its holster. My heart set up a pounding inside my chest. I strained at the rope, trying to get free, trying to move out of line of the gun.

Ben let off six shots, one after the other, so quick the sound of each one overlapped the last, like a chain of noise; and the echoes strung out and vibrated through the forest. Bullets rammed into the tree all round my head, thumping into the wood like hammer blows, sending splinters flying. The noise of it all deafened me. When it was over, I found myself standing stiff as a steel pole, my eyes shut tight as vices.

When I looked again, Ben was sitting on his horse, one knee resting on his saddle horn, laughing and shouting to George:

'Just look at that boy wince, brother George!'

George was barely smiling. 'You've had your fun. Let's go,' I heard him say.

'I don't hold with shooting defenceless boys,' Ben

shouted. 'But next time either my brother or I see you on our trail you'll get a bullet right between your eyes.'

He turned and jogged off after George, and I could hear his laughter long after they were out of sight.

6

After a time, my head stopped spinning, and my legs felt they had bones in them instead of running water. But the calmer I became, the more foolish I felt, strapped to a tree without my boots on. And my pride was hurt. I got to calling myself all the insulting names I could think of for letting myself be caught like that. I cursed Ben, and my misfortune, and my stupidity. I got as far as thinking I deserved to be tied up for not keeping my wits about me!

But I soon got bored with thinking such things. The ropes were so tight my arms were starting to hurt like they do when you sleep on them too long.

I called for Silva, and whistled. But all that did was scare the birds. They flew up screaming their danger signals, filling the air with raucous noise till they got on my nerves and I gave up.

If Silva heard, he would come. I waited, but he didn't appear. And that made me feel lonely. Why, I thought suddenly, I'm a sitting prey. I had heard people talk about bears in the mountains, and I'd seen mountain lions myself, roaming the hills. Tied as I was, without boots on my feet, I didn't stand a chance against even a lynx or a wolverine.

I listened to every sound; and every sound set my eyes searching to find what made it. Soon I was starting at every flutter of a bird in the leaves, every creak of a

branch in the breeze. One time I nearly jumped out of my skin when a raccoon went by. He sniffed at me and looked me over with his sad, black-ringed eyes and went on.

I didn't hear the rattlesnake coming. My eye caught its movement among the undergrowth: grass heads rocking sharply where it was, and quiet again at once when it had passed. And the jittering grass showed it was coming right at me. About eight feet away it came into view, the waving line of its body hugging the ground. Sweat broke out on my forehead; the blood drained from me. People say snakes fix their eyes on their victims and hypnotise them. But that isn't what freezes you to the spot: it is fear. I watched that rattlesnake come closer and closer, flicking its forked tongue, and the only thing I knew was that if it stopped and coiled itself in front of me and gave a rattle with its tail, I was done for.

It got within striking distance of me when, unthinking, I swung my legs upwards and held them as high as I could. The tightness of the rope supported my body.

The rattler writhed past without so much as a glance.

My legs dropped like felled trees, and hung limply, unable to take the weight of my body. I slumped, held up by the rope, panting.

Suddenly, all I wanted was sleep. Sleep and food and water: sweet, clear, ice-cold mountain water. And to be free from the cutting pain of the ropes.

I was lying flat on the ground, being rubbed on the arms. My eyes cleared and looked into a man's greying stubbled beard.

'Jake!' I said, and tried to get up. But my arms wouldn't move: they were just weights, without feeling.

'You lie there,' Jake said. He lifted my head and tipped

water into my mouth from his water bottle.

'Knew you'd get yourself into some kind of mess,' he said. 'So I sent Charlie Stephens to fetch the sheriff from Pinedale, and came after you soon as I could. Took me a time to pick up your trail, night being so close and all. But soon as I saw the direction you were taking, I says to myself, "Jake, there's but one place them Shaws is making for. . . ." '

'Jackson,' I said.

'Right!' said Jake.

'I heard them talking last night.'

'Didn't take no eavesdropping to tell that, son. I was plumb stupid not to think of it before. Well, anyways, I kept trailing this morning, and before long I met up with your nag running loose. Knew there was trouble ahead. I found you a few minutes back, with that rope so tight your blood could hardly move.'

My arms were full of tingling pains now, and feeling they might burst. But my head was clearing.

I was glad to see Jake: told him all that had happened, he following the tale with soundless whistles through the gaps in his teeth, and scratchings of his beard, and shakings of his head.

'That's a mean-minded pair,' he said when I finished.

I stood up, swaying a little from dizziness and the weakness of my legs. Jake had Silva tethered alongside his own horse. I went to him, and checked him over. He had done himself no harm, and the way he nuzzled at my shoulder, I guessed he was as happy to see me as I was to have him back.

'We've got to get you a good meal, and a night of sleep,' Jake said.

I leaned against Silva. I had a mind to argue, but not the

strength. 'It riles me to think of those Shaws getting free.'

'I thought maybe you'd learned not to meddle with those two again,' Jake said. 'You've done what you could. A man can't do any more. Up to the sheriff now, son.'

He helped me mount, and rode ahead.

'Reckon the best thing is to make for Horse Creek. There's some homesteaders in the valley above Merna. Maybe one of them will fix us up. Nearer to there than we are to home.'

I didn't object. Horse Creek was farther up the trail the way the Shaws had gone.

It was dark by the time we reached the creek. We followed it down a stretch till we saw a light shining from a cabin window.

Jake knocked at the door when we got there. A man holding a lamp answered. Jake talked with him a while. As they talked, a woman came to the door and looked out at me; and then a girl I judged to be about sixteen or seventeen looked out too.

At last all four of them came fussing up to me. The man held Silva's head while Jake helped me off. They were going over and over the details of what happened, repeating it all. The woman tried to help Jake, and clucked away at me, calling me 'Poor boy' and oh-ing and ah-ing about my bootless feet, and how exhausted I was, and what devils some men were. The girl stood and watched. I looked at her and smiled at the goings-on. She flushed at that. She was a mighty pretty girl: thin, with long fair hair loose round her shoulders, as though she had just let it down ready for going to bed.

I was got inside, all the time treated as though I was at death's door. Wasn't till we were inside that people thought of mentioning names. So there followed a round of introductions, and everybody got embarrassed like people do when they have to tell their names.

The folks were called Turner: Dan and Jane. The girl was their daughter, Betsy. She said 'Hello' when her mother told us that, and flushed again, and said, 'I'll go and make up a bed, Ma,' and went rushing out of the room.

'Thought the days when this kind of thing happened were over hereabouts,' Dan Turner said. 'Thought a man and his family was safe. Seems it ain't so.'

Jake and Dan chewed over that theme for a while. Mrs Turner set to, laying the table, and tending pans on the fire, and coming to me now and then and looking at me, feeling my brow and clucking her tongue.

It was all just the funniest sight, all the fuss and solemn talk; but I didn't laugh out loud. I reckoned they were too old to understand what was so comic.

One thing I'll say for Mrs Turner: she cooked better than most anyone I'd met. In next to no time, she had a meal on the table that made my mouth water just looking at it. Jake and I set to eating our way through piled-up plates of stewed beef and corn bread and pickles, with steaming mugs of coffee that would have pleased the heart of any range-riding cowman: hot as hell, black as sin, and strong as death.

Dan Turner talked while we ate. 'If those two are making for Jackson,' he said, 'they've some pretty rugged country to get through. Might just be they'll take longer than they think.'

'Don't see how anyone can catch them now, even so,' I said between bites.

'I'm not so sure,' Dan said. 'If I was wanting to avoid people I wouldn't travel the usual trails.'

'They aren't,' I said. 'Otherwise they wouldn't have gone so high up the mountains.'

'Still,' Jake said, stew gravy running through his beard, 'there's only one pass to Jackson from here. Hoback Canyon.'

'Not so,' Dan said. 'That's the way most folk take across the Divide. It's the easiest pass. But there's another route. The early settlers used it before the Hoback was found. Down Little Greys River and north up Snake River. It's longer and its more difficult. But nowadays it's safer for folk who want to keep hidden.'

Dan got up and filled a pipe from a tobacco bowl that stood on the window ledge. Jake and I went on eating. Nobody said much more just then: but it was easy to see we were thinking hard.

We finished supper, and Jake and I thanked Mrs Turner good and proper. Dan brought me a pair of his boots. His feet were bigger than mine, but Mrs Turner stuffed some cotton wool into the toes till they fitted snug.

I felt refreshed, and wanted time to think: I somehow felt that there was a way to do something about the Shaws, if only I could hit on it.

'I'm just going to check Silva,' I said. 'Won't take a minute.'

'You should be in bed, young Clint,' Mrs Turner said. 'After the time you've had.'

I laughed. 'Feel fine, Mrs Turner. Thanks to your dinner.'

She was pleased at that. 'Somebody has to look after you men,' she said. 'Seems it's more than you can do for yourselves.'

Jake flashed me a look. 'No fancy games,' he said.

'It's all right, Jake,' I said. 'I ain't going to chase after the Shaws!'

He looked at Dan. 'Just the stubbornest young creature I ever did see!' he said. Dan laughed, and I left them to their old men's talk.

7

It was warmer than the night before, without a stir of wind. The moon shone clear in the sky, so bright I could see the snow on the mountains. There was a coyote howling away off in the trees.

Dan Turner had put Silva in a small corral at the back of the cabin, where he kept some horses of his own. I leaned on the corral fence and clucked my tongue quietly. Silva detached himself from the dark group of grazing horses and trotted to me. I patted him and talked softly to him.

I heard a step behind me and turned my head. It was Betsy. She came to the fence and stroked Silva's neck.

'He's a nice-looking horse,' she said.

'Thanks,' I said.

She laughed. 'I wasn't complimenting you!'

'Like my horse, like me!' I said.

She laughed again. 'What's his name?'

'Silva.'

'Is he one of your father's or is he really yours?'

'Mine. Got him for my fourteenth birthday,' I said. 'Four years ago.'

That seemed to end the conversation. I strained for something more to say, but nothing came. It's just the silliest feeling: wanting to talk to a pretty girl and finding nothing to say. I got to thinking that one of the troubles with living on an out-of-the-way place like Pa's was that I never saw many girls of any kind – pretty or ugly. Didn't get the practice of talking with them!

We stood a while side by side, the horse's head between us. Betsy went on petting Silva; I went on thinking about having nothing to say. Then that darned animal trotted off and went back to grazing, leaving me tongue-tied with Betsy.

I eyed her, hoping she might come up with something, but she just stared at the sky, and the jagged line of the mountains, till I got embarrassed with the silence.

I coughed and hitched my levis.

'I suppose you're thinking about how to stop those men?' Betsy said, and it came out all in a rush.

'Well – I don't aim to let them get away if I can help it,' I said.

'Mr Barnes is afraid you'll go off and do something, well . . . he said, do something stupid!'

'Did he tell you that?'

'No, he said it to my pa.' Betsy paused a minute. 'But he did ask me to come out here.'

'He did *what*?' I said.

'He asked Pa if I could come out and keep you company because he was afraid you'd rush off and do something stupid if you were left alone.'

I couldn't help laughing. 'Why that two-timing son of a cowhand!' I said.

'Did you plan to do something?' she said.

'Haven't got a plan at all yet. I came out to think about it.'

I started walking round the corral. Betsy followed a step behind.

'Mr Barnes is right: you'll only get hurt,' she said.

'You go along with the rest of them, eh? You think the

Shaws should be left to play their jokes and murder a few people here and there?'

'No. But you can't take on those two single-handed. You don't even carry a gun.'

'What's your plan, then?'

'Leave them to the sheriff.'

I said mocking, 'Jake is the sheriff!'

Betsy pushed me from behind. 'You *are* stubborn, like Jake says!'

She was standing with her hands on her hips, her feet astride. I faced her and stood the same way.

'Go for your guns!' I said.

She laughed then. 'But you know what I mean,' she said.

'I know,' I said. 'Which is what bothers me too.' We walked on, circling the corral slowly side by side. 'They're all muscle and sharp shooting, the Shaws. Seems to me, the only way to tackle that kind of thing is by using your head: brain against brawn – that kind of thing. Only my brain isn't as good as their brawn, and it ain't as fast as their shooting.'

'Why, it is!' Betsy said.

'Well, thank you, Miss Turner!' I said, very courtly.

She looked down at her feet. 'I don't like to think you might get hurt,' she said, 'that's why I said you should wait for the sheriff.'

'All I aim to do is hold the Shaws up till the sheriff gets there. Another day and they'll be in reach of Jackson. Nobody will catch them then, and the sheriff won't get on their trail till tomorrow.'

There's nothing better for raising a man's spirits than talking to a pretty girl who is a good listener, and soon I felt encouraged. Before I knew it, I was talking enough to crack my jaw. I told Betsy all about my folks and how the trouble started. And I went over the happenings since then. I didn't add too much, either – just a detail here and there to help the story along. Betsy was the easiest person to talk to. She listened attentive as a man could wish for; and she laughed and sympathised in the right places, and didn't interrupt all through.

There's some folk you meet one minute, and the next minute you feel you've known them all your life. Everything fits: you're relaxed and easy and happy as a prairie lark in summer. It was like that with Betsy and me. Hadn't happened to me before. Made me light-headed, I suppose, and soon my imagination invented the wildest plans for ambushing the Shaws. Mostly the plans were so far-fetched they ended up being funny. So Betsy and I spent half an hour giggling together.

Suddenly, out of all that fanciful thinking, I had a thought. I remembered what Dan Turner said during supper about the two ways through to Jackson. Suppose the brothers *had* followed the old trail. Then, if Jake and I set off as early as could be tomorrow and went through Hoback Canyon, we might beat the brothers to the spot where the Hoback and Snake River meet. And if we could do that, we might be able to hold them there long enough for the sheriff to reach us.

'Betsy,' I said, cutting off in the middle of one of the flights of fancy, 'I think I've got a plan.'

I explained it to her, my words keeping just ahead of my thoughts.

Betsy got as excited as a kitten with a ball of wool. 'Why, Clint,' she cried, 'I know that place. You could hold them up there easy. The gorge is narrow, and there's places to take cover.'

I let out a whoop. 'I think we've got it, Betsy.'

'And Pa could ride over to Calpet and let the sheriff know where you'd gone. That way, he could make straight for you and save time searching out your trail.'

I was overjoyed. I took her hands and swung her round. She stumbled about laughing and tripping over her skirts, and shrieking out for me to stop. When I did, she hung on to me, dizzy.

Then both at once we realised we were so close that I could feel her body panting. She was warm and soft. Standing together like that was just the most pleasant thing I could think of. And she didn't try to move away.

'Take care,' she said.

'I aim to,' I said.

'On the way back . . .' she said.

'I'll call in for supper,' I said.

She laughed.

'Now all we have to do is persuade Jake,' I said.

Jake thought of every reason in the world why the plan wouldn't work. We'd be too late. We would be outgunned. I might get hurt and he'd be responsible. We hadn't enough ammunition. The longer he went on, the shorter my temper became. The more reasons he thought up, the more determined I was to do what I'd planned. Finally, I got so angry I burst out:

'I'm sorry for you, Jake Barnes!'

The talking stopped; everyone looked at me.

'You're just an old man who's scared,' I said, shaking. 'You've taken that deputy's badge and you've taken the money that goes with it. But you're just too darned scared to do what that badge says you swore to do. You're going to let them two outlaws get clear away, and you haven't even got a conscience about it.'

There was the kind of shock in the room that happens when somebody has said something harsh. Jake sat glowering at me; Dan Turner leaned forward in his chair, his elbows resting on his knees, and hung his head; Mrs Turner looked close to tears; Betsy put a hand on my arm, as though to stop me. But I went on.

'I'll tell you something, Jake. You can do what you want. But soon as light shows tomorrow morning, I'm taking off after them brothers.'

There was a heavy pause. Nobody moved. Nobody looked at anyone else. With the words out of me, my anger cooled. I felt a little ashamed then, but I was still too stirred up to apologise. Anyway, I'd said what I thought, and I couldn't see any use in apologising for that.

Mr Turner shifted in his seat, then stood up.

'Time we all went to bed,' he said, quiet and calm. 'We're all tired. Things will look better in the morning.'

He went to Betsy and put his arm round her, guiding her towards the door. Mrs Turner went round the room, tidying. Jake sat still a moment, then stood up slowly, his hands pushing on the table to help his old man's legs.

'Clint's right,' he said.

'Now, Jake,' Dan Turner said, stopping and facing him. 'Clint needs some rest. He didn't mean what he said.'

'No, he's right,' Jake said. 'I've known that since yesterday. It's been grinding away at my belly ever since I let him go out of town on his own.' He looked at me and smiled, and scratched his beard. 'You'd think when a body gets as old as me, he'd have learned a thing or two about the way a man should live. And care less about how he dies. Well . . . seems like it's the other way about.'

'I'm sorry, Jake,' I said. 'I didn't mean to speak out at you like that. . . .'

He lifted his hand to stop me.

'There ain't no apology needed, Clint,' he said. 'You was right.'

There was a silence again. Nobody knew what to say next.

Then Jake scratched his beard. 'Well,' he said, bluff as his old self. 'If we're to get any sleep at all tonight, we'd better plan a few things about the morning.'

Dan Turner smiled. 'Better put that coffee pot back on the stove, Jane,' he said.

8

We were up before first light. We had sat up so late, none of us got enough sleep; our eyes were heavy, and Jake, Dan and I sat down to breakfast, silent and glum. Mrs Turner hustled about, her hair still in rag curlers, and told us to eat more.

'You've a long day ahead of you – you'll be glad of a good meal.'

I was aching all over my body. Where the ropes had cut into me, I was sore and bruised. And thinking about ambushing the brothers made me excited and nervous both at once so that my stomach was tight, and I couldn't eat much of what Mrs Turner put in front of me. All I wanted was to get on.

After breakfast, in the early dawn light, we saddled up, filled the water bottles, and packed some food. The fresh morning air, blowing cold from the mountains, woke me up, and it was good to be moving. The three of us went over the plan again while we worked. Jake and I were to try and hold up the brothers at Snake River. Dan was to ride to Calpet, find the sheriff and bring him to the river as fast as he could.

The sun stood on the horizon when we mounted in front of the cabin. It was so bright we were squinting at each other, our hats pulled down to shade our eyes.

Betsy ran out of the cabin just then, her hair still

tousled from sleep, and a shawl wrapped round her nightdress. She looked just the most beautiful thing I ever saw. She came up to me, and she was carrying a gun: a Winchester repeater.

'Take this, Clint,' she said. 'There's only Jake's rifle between you. That isn't enough. This is Pa's. He said I could offer it to you.'

I hesitated. It was the strangest thing: I didn't agree with my pa about guns. Seemed to me a man had a right to defend himself. But all my life, since I was old enough to listen, he'd impressed on me that guns were the weapons of the Devil, and how I was never to use one against another man, nor against animals either, if I could help it. 'A man that carries a gun means to use it,' he'd say, 'and men that use guns, die by guns. Guns breed killing – that's the long and the short of it.' There'd been times I'd argued; and times he'd lost his temper. Even so, now I was offered one, I drew back as though it would be letting him down to take it.

Betsy saw me hesitate. 'Your pa?' she said.

I nodded.

'Seems to me you made your choice when you came after the Shaws.' She spoke quietly, but there was an edge to her voice that cut. 'Besides – we want you to come back,' she said.

I took the Winchester and the spare ammunition she handed up with it. 'I'll be back,' I said. 'In time for supper.'

She smiled; then joined her mother, standing in the cabin door. They looked cosy and warm, bathed in the sunlight. The horses in the corral grazed, peaceful, swishing their tails at the flies, and the Turners' few hens clucked about their feet.

I looked at Jake and Dan, and saw they too were taking in the scene and feeling like me, I expect: it was real and good and how things should be. And us riding off was some kind of dream. A dream you know might turn into a nightmare, but that you can't prevent.

We wheeled the horses round and rode away from the cabin, waving to the women in the doorway, but did not shout goodbyes.

We rode hard, and by noon were in Hoback Canyon. The mountains rose sharply on either side, and the going was tough. Tough on the horses; tough on the men. Silva shone with sweat. Behind me, I could hear Jake panting hard, and sometimes groaning when his old man's bones were shaken. But he never complained, and somehow kept his horse working.

An hour later we reached Snake River. The mountains folded together, covered in tall pines. The river wound along the valley just the way it should with such a name. It was shallow, and the water surged and swirled, and curled over white where boulders and rock broke the surface.

We halted on a rise to catch our breath and take in the terrain. If our thinking was right, and we had managed to reach here before the brothers, they would come upstream. The pines covered the area so thickly it was difficult to pick out a place that was protected, yet commanded a view of the river bank.

Jake was looking steadily downstream. He took off his hat and held it close to his head, shading his face from the sun. He had seen something, but I couldn't see what. He lifted his hand and pointed.

'Over that next spur,' he said. 'See it?'

I screwed up my eyes and stared. Nothing: just pines, and hills rising beyond, and blue sky so bright it dazzled.

'What?'

'Smoke,' Jake said.

I held my hat as he did. And saw it: a thin wisp of grey, like a twist of rope.

'Trappers?' I said.

'Could be,' Jake said. 'We'd best know who.'

He turned his horse downhill. We reached the river and worked our way downstream in the direction of the smoke. We said nothing. Jake kept the pace slow, his eyes raised, searching the way ahead, while his horse picked out its own trail.

From the next rise, the smoke was clear. It was coming from a point half a mile or so down river, but still hidden by the trees. We pushed on, but now Jake rode with his rifle laid across his saddle, his right hand covering the trigger.

About a quarter of a mile from where we judged the smoke to be coming from, we dismounted and tethered the horses.

'Can't take any chances,' Jake said. 'Might be them, might not.'

We took the guns and walked on, following the path of the river, but keeping among the trees.

At last we came to a clearing about a hundred yards long and fifty wide, edged by the river, and the forest curving round. A one-room cabin stood in it. The front was angled to the river. From where we stood hidden in the trees, we could see the front and one side. The glass had gone from the two windows on either side of the door. The roof had lost some of its covering, and grass grew on the rest. Weathered roof timbers showed in the gaps. The chimney was stone-built on the forest side, and from it came the smoke we had seen.

We waited a while. Nobody appeared.

'Trapper's cabin,' Jake said. 'Pretty old one too. Ain't been used for quite a time.'

'Well, there's someone in there now, Jake.'

'Yeh,' said Jake. 'But who? Don't get many trappers round here nowadays.'

Silence again. Not a sound, but the river and birds and Jake's breathing, heavy from the walk through the forest. Not a movement: except that smoke rising.

'Well, it ain't any good just waiting here, Jake.'

'There you go again!' Jake said. 'Always rushing to do something. We've got to know who's in there before anything else.'

'Tell you what, Jake,' I said. 'You stay here out of sight. Keep the cabin covered. I'll take a look at the back of the cabin: see what I can see.'

'Then just you be careful, you hear me?'

'I'll watch myself, Jake. Anything happens, you blaze away with that rifle of yours.'

I went back into the forest a way, then struck out on a path that would take me round the clearing so that I could come at the cabin from the back. When I judged I'd gone far enough, I listened for the river and made towards it.

As soon as the cabin came in sight, I stopped. Two horses were tethered behind it. They were big beasts, with red and white Navaho blankets under their saddles. They were the Shaw horses all right.

I looked across the clearing at the place where Jake was hidden. I couldn't see a sign of him. I took another glance at the cabin. There was one small window in the back wall, but no door. The logs were rough-hewn, and the

mud filling had come away in places, leaving gaps between them. There was a pile of small sticks stacked against the wall, and an old water barrel beside it with the hoops gone and the wood planks broken.

I was on the point of going back when I felt something about the cabin had changed. There had been no noise or movement, but my instinct made me look again.

The smoke from the chimney had stopped. High in the air a small white cloud of it drifted away downriver on the breeze, and there was no longer the thin twist of smoke rising from the cabin.

Someone had doused the fire: suddenly doused it, with a bowl of water or, more likely, with the dregs from a pot of coffee, the way cowhands douse their fires when they break camp. And that could mean only one thing: the brothers were moving on.

George Shaw appeared just then, coming round the cabin from the front, carrying a saddle bag. He strapped the bag to his horse, checked the girth, and went back round the cabin.

There was no time to reach Jake. While the brothers had those horses, there was a chance for them to get away as soon as the shooting started. They couldn't ride off straight by Jake towards Jackson, but they *could* make a dash for the forest on the other side of the clearing and circle round us. While they were in the cabin, we had them held down. And that was what we wanted. It was clear as daylight what I had to do: those horses had to be got rid of.

I needed both hands, so I laid my rifle behind a tree. Then, crouching low, I ran as fast as I could towards the back of the cabin. There was about twenty yards of clearing to cover, and I reckoned Jake would see me for

half that distance. He'd know something was up. Funny thing was, as I ran I thought of Jake cussing and muttering about me getting up to fool tricks again!

I reached the horses without anything happening. I took the halter of the first, and mounted the second. And dug him hard as I could with my spurs. The horse bucked, and let out a wild neigh. Then took off at a gallop. I hung on and kept a tight grip on the halter of the trailing horse. I lay flat to the horse's neck, and was halfway back across the clearing before the first bullet whined past me. Two more shots cracked off behind me right after the first. Then, from over the clearing, came the loud, deep, punching sound of a rifle. Jake had opened up.

9

In the cover of the trees, I picked up my gun and circled round towards Jake. He had drawn the brothers' fire, and the shots were ringing back and forth.

I tethered the horses out of danger of the flying lead and ran, crouching, to Jake's side. Bullets ricocheted in the trees, fetching leaves down on our heads, and splitting open the bark of the trees round us. Thick amber sap ran down from the splits like blood from wounds.

'What d'you think you're doing?' Jake growled.

'Horse rustling,' I said. Now we had the brothers cornered, and the shooting had started, I was excited, like a hunter when he sights his prey.

'Huh!' Jake said. He let off a round from his carbine. 'What d'you want to go stirring up this hornets' nest for? Everything was quiet and cosy till you went dashing about playing the hero. Near gave me heart failure.'

I aimed at one of the cabin windows and fired the Winchester.

'They were leaving,' I said. 'Had to do something.'

Jake's hat spun off and flopped to his side. He picked it up, dusted it off, and looked at the bullet hole newly made in the crown.

'Now look at that,' he said sadly, 'as though the darned thing weren't draughty enough.' He replaced his hat, let go two rapidly fired rounds from his carbine, and dodged back behind the tree. 'Life won't be worth living round here soon.'

'Just keep banging away at them, Jake, and we've got them held tight.'

Two more shots from the cabin whistled over us.

'And just how long d'you think we can keep this up?' Jake said. His face was shining with sweat. 'And just how long will it be before a piece of lead knocks a hole in one of us?' He leaned round the trunk and fired. And bobbed back. 'And just how long d'you think the ammunition is going to last?'

'Till the sheriff gets here, I hope,' I said.

Two more shots from the cabin: two more bullets whined by; two more shots from Jake and me answered them.

'Sheriff could be a while yet,' Jake said. He looked at the sun. 'There's maybe three hours of light left. Then what?'

I pondered. Jake was right. If the sheriff didn't get here by dusk, the Shaws would have darkness to cover them, and they would be off. The rate of fire had died down already. The brothers would be thinking just the same thing as us: save ammunition, wait until dark, and make a dash for it. Time was on their side.

'We'll have to flush them out into the open,' I said.

Jake screwed up his eyes at me, and scratched his beard. 'Can't you ever think of something quiet and safe for a change?'

'Don't know about you, Jake,' I said. 'But I don't care much for lying here giving the Shaws target practice.'

I was lying flat, my head pressed against the base of the tree, and my gun was aimed for firing. Something wet touched my cheek. I rubbed it off, and found my fingers sticky with sap which had run down from the bullet wounds high up the trunk. It was this that gave me the idea.

'Jake,' I said, 'I've got a plan.'

'I've had enough of your plans, young Clint,' Jake said. 'You just give the Shaws a bullet or two to think about, and that will do for the present.'

But between our times of firing at the Shaws and ducking from their shots, I told Jake what I had in mind.

'Won't work,' Jake said. 'It's too risky.'

'You just keep the brothers busy,' I said. 'And remember what I told you.' Then before Jake could stop me, I set off into the trees.

'Doggone it! He's off again!' I heard him mutter. But he was too busy answering the brothers' fire to do more.

I crawled back out of sight and range of the cabin, and looked about for a dry stick and soon found one: three feet long or so, and as thick as my wrist. Then I found a young pine, and stripped the bark from a section, prising it away with my knife. Between the bark and the wood of the tree the sap was thick and fresh. The spring rise, it's called: the time when the sap flows fastest, reviving the tree after winter.

I took off my neckerchief, and tore it into lengths about four inches wide. I rubbed these into the sap, then tied them in layers round one end of my stick. When I had finished, my hands were brown from the sap, and its sweet smell was strong.

Next I went to the Shaw horses and searched the saddle bags. I found what I wanted: matches wrapped in oilskin to keep them dry. The Shaws were old hands at living rough: they wouldn't have forgotten either the matches or the wrapping.

Carrying my stick and gun, I rode one of the horses through the forest, circling the cabin again, to the spot I'd reached before. All this while bursts of gunfire told me everything was as I left it. I tethered the horse out of sight but near enough to reach if I needed him quickly, and crept to the edge of the clearing, where there was a large boulder. It gave me good protection, and was just at the right point for doing what I planned.

Jake was about seventy yards away, in front and to my right. I could see the burst of gunsmoke each time he fired. I prepared myself for setting off the plan. Once it was begun, there would be no stopping till the Shaws were caught. Or dead.

I aimed my rifle for the back window of the cabin. From this angle, the bullet wouldn't hit anybody. But I didn't want that. All I wanted was to get them worried. I pulled the trigger, reloaded and pulled again.

There was a pause in the shooting, just as I expected. The Shaws would be organising themselves to take care of the new development. I crouched behind the boulder.

Pistol fire – all six shots from a full chamber – spread wild and wide into the forest round me. I grinned to myself. They were worried! There was Jake in front of them, and now a gun behind. And they weren't sure where the new shot came from.

Another pause. The Shaws would be watching for more shots from the back of the cabin so as to locate the position they came from. This was Jake's opportunity.

'You Shaws,' Jake shouted, his voice sounding hollow across the clearing. 'You hear me? This is the law. We have you covered. I'm going to give you three minutes to come out of there with your hands high. After that, you take your chance. Starting now.'

Silence, but for the river and the breeze stirring in the trees. They were soft and peaceful sounds after the gunfire. And yet they made me nervous too: while the guns were talking, I knew what was happening. In this silence there was no way of knowing just what the brothers were up to.

I crouched behind the boulder, and looked cautiously at the cabin. There was nothing new to see. It was a noise that came unexpectedly. It seemed at first to be mingled with the sound of the river; but as it grew louder I knew it came from the cabin. I lifted my head higher. The sound was voices raised. The Shaws' voices. And they weren't answering Jake. They were arguing.

I strained to catch the words, but the cabin walls and the wind muffled them. They grew louder still, and the louder they were, the more angry they became.

Suddenly the voices ceased. The hair on the back of my neck prickled.

'Sheriff.' The voice was George Shaw's. I picked up my rifle and aimed for the cabin. 'I'm coming out.'

'Keep your hands high in the air,' Jake shouted.

George came into view a few feet in front of the cabin. He was walking slowly, his hands up.

A shot cracked. Dust puffed from the back of George's vest. His body lurched forward, jerked, and fell heavily, face down, to the ground.

10

I could not take my eyes from George's body. Blood spread from the wound in his back. I stared, thinking at first that Jake had shot him. Then, in a kind of horror, I knew that Ben had fired the bullet.

'Hey, sheriff.'

I heard Ben's voice, but my eyes and mind could not break away from the sight of George lying slumped on the ground.

'You've been misled. Us Shaws don't give in to the law. We ain't ever been caught. We ain't ever going to be. Not alive!'

He laughed: laughed like he had when I struggled with George in Joe's saloon; and like he had after the shooting in the forest. And I knew he'd laughed like that when he shot the rope that held my pa. It was a wild, high-pitched, crazy sound.

'You want me, sheriff, you come and get me.'

He let fly a volley of shots. Only then did I break from the trance that held me. I got back behind the boulder. But something inside me had changed. The excitement had gone. I felt sick in my stomach, and a weary blankness in my mind.

Shots cracked from the cabin, and every one was like a blow from a man's fist on my ears. And every blow built fury in me at the man who made it. And blow on blow turned fury to hate, until at last I could think no more.

I grabbed the stick, and fingered for the matches in my pocket. I lit a match and held it to the cloth. It flamed up at once, the sap working like fuel, burning hot and smokeless.

I held the torch away from me with my left hand, and with my right fired the rifle into the sky. That was Jake's signal. He sent a stream of bullets into the cabin.

I stood, ran clear of the trees, and hurled the torch toward the back of the cabin. It whirled in the air, arching, a trail of vapour marking its path. I was under cover before it landed.

When I looked again, I felt a kind of pleasure : the torch had landed plumb on the pile of sticks, and flame was already spreading among them.

If Ben made a dash for it, he would head for the downriver trail away from Jake. So I worked my way through the trees until I met the trail, then came back to the edge of the clearing.

The back of the cabin was well alight. Smoke billowed up, rising straight till it topped the trees, where the breeze angled it. It drifted overhead in a grey cloud, and the noise of crackling wood and heat came with it.

Flames climbed on to the roof and spread rapidly over it. The shooting from the cabin stopped. For a time there was only the noise and smell of burning wood, the sun-red flames bright against the green pines.

Suddenly a gust of wind eddied round the clearing. The smoke curled back on itself, and blew round the cabin like mist.

A broken roof spar crashed, burning into the cabin. Sparks danced. Smoke gusted from the windows and the cracks in the walls.

'Sheriff!' Ben shouted, and his voice choked with smoke. The door flung open.

'Sheriff. I'm coming out.'

Ben ran into the open. His hands covered his face; he stumbled and his chest heaved, gasping for air.

'Hold it there,' Jake shouted.

Ben halted, feet apart. To his right George lay, and behind him only the front wall of the cabin was free of flames. The rest burned now so fiercely that there was little smoke, and tongues of fire leapt skywards.

Jake stood and walked out of the trees, his rifle waist-high, pointed at Ben.

'Throw down your gun,' he called.

Ben's hand went to his gun in its holster, and slowly lifted it clear. His arm swung, as though to throw the gun in front of him. But it did not stop swinging. And the gun never left it. It came suddenly and very fast upwards, and fired. Almost in the same movement, Ben flung himself to his right and rolled over George's body.

Jake staggered, took two steps forward; tried to raise his rifle.

I ran towards him.

Ben fired again.

Jake's gun dropped from him and his hands went to his chest. He opened his mouth and cried out:

'Clint . . .'

He reeled backwards, and the cry died on his lips as he fell.

'Jake . . .' I shouted.

Pain cut through my right shoulder, and the crack of Ben's pistol came with it. I was spun round by the blow of the bullet.

There was no more thought then, no more knowing.

The world was red. There was only rage and flame and dying sun. And in my hands the gun fired shot after shot at the huddle of bodies that were George and Ben.

Then there was the click-click-click of the trigger, and no kick-back from exploding bullets.

And there were flames leaping higher: the cabin shaped in fire that roared. And a sheet of flame that was the front wall fell, hissing through the air, and covered the huddled bodies.

Sparks and smoke and heat came in a wave across the clearing, burning, choking, forcing me back, stumbling, coughing. But still the click-click-click from the gun in my hands. Until trees stood in my eyes and blocked from my sight the clearing and the flames over the bodies.

I could not look again till the blinding rage died in me.

The smoke had lifted. There was nothing left of the cabin but charred and burning spars of wood criss-crossed in piles. Only the chimney stood, a blackened memorial to what had been there. I felt at once so weary, so desolate, so alone, I wanted to run from the place. I stood among the trees, the gun hanging in my hands, and for a long time I could do nothing but stare across the clearing, stunned.

Slowly there drifted back to me the sound of the river. I noticed then that the sun had dropped behind the mountain peaks, and shadows round me were deep in the twilight. I felt the pain in my arm for the first time. I looked and saw the shirt on my right shoulder was soaked with blood, but I felt no wish to tend it.

I walked into the clearing and crossed to where Jake's body lay, twisted just as he had fallen. Blood covered his chest. His eyes stared in the surprise of his death. His mouth was open as though it would still finish its cry.

It seemed indecent to leave him like that. I went to the Shaw horse, took its saddle blanket and covered Jake's body.

I wanted to do more for him. But there was nothing now except to wait until the sheriff came.

He rode in not long after with a posse, and Dan Turner, as the last light of sunset reddened the sky. They reined in their horses at the edge of the clearing, and their eyes passed over the wreckage of the cabin, and the covered body, and me standing by it. No one moved or said anything. Then the sheriff dismounted and walked to me.

'Jake?' he asked, looking at the covered body. I nodded. 'Did you get the Shaws?'

I pointed at the smouldering wood. 'Over there,' I said.

The sheriff went to the charred wreckage, and began poking about in it with his feet. He turned and called the men, and they ran across. They started speaking then, their voices quiet and full of questions.

Dan Turner stopped by me.

'Sorry we couldn't make it here sooner, Clint,' he said.

'Me too,' I said.

The men round the wreckage went silent.

One of them turned to us and shouted, 'We've found them.'

The talking broke out again, more high-pitched with excitement.

Another man saw us watching and called, 'You did a great job, Clint,' and smiled, and turned back, bending over the place where the bodies were.

'Mr Turner,' I said, 'I'll be glad to get out of here.'

Dan looked at me, and nodded.

'Reckon you can make it to my place?' he said.

'I'll make it,' I said.

DISTRICT LIBRARY